The Pledge of Allegiance

by Kristine
Lombardi Frankel
illustrated by
Susanna Rumiz

SCHOLASTIC INC.

ISBN 978-1-338-28198-9

10 9 8 7 6 5 4 3 2 1   18 19 20 21 22

Printed in the U.S.A.   40
This edition first printing 2018

Book design by Jennifer Rinaldi

Something to Think About

Did you know . . .

• The Pledge of Allegiance was first published
in 1892 in a magazine called *The Youth's Companion*.

• The Pledge of Allegiance was first recited in schools on October 12, 1892,
the 400th anniversary of Columbus's arrival in the Americas.

• The first line originally began: "I pledge allegiance to my flag."
In 1923, the words "my flag" were changed to "the flag of the United States."
In 1924, the words "of America" were added.

• Congress officially recognized the Pledge of Allegiance in 1942.

• In 1954, Congress added the words "under God" to the pledge.

"Good morning, class," says Ms. Francis.
"Today we have a new student. This is Linda.
Linda just moved to the United States."

"Hi, Linda!"

"Let's show Linda how we start each day," says Ms. Francis.

"We come in when the bell rings and sit in our seats," Pam begins. "Ms. Francis takes attendance and makes announcements."

"Then we say the Pledge of Allegiance together," Elizabeth explains.

"We stand with our right hands
over our hearts to say the
Pledge of Allegiance," Tommy adds.

"Let's say the Pledge of Allegiance together," says Ms. Francis. "And let's take turns explaining to Linda what it means."

"I pledge allegiance . . ."

"That means we promise to be loyal," says Tony.

"to the flag . . ."

"The flag has thirteen stripes and fifty stars," says Mia.

"of the United States of America . . ."

"Our country started with thirteen states,
and now it has fifty states," explains Patrick.

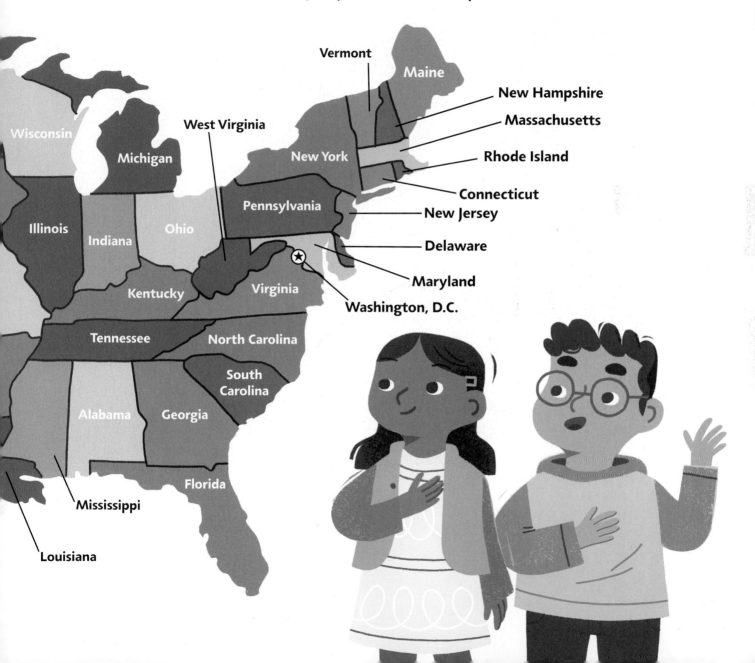

"and to the Republic . . ."

"A republic is a country where the people vote to elect their government leaders," says Rose.

"for which it stands . . ."

"The flag stands for the United States. It's the symbol of our country," says Richard.

"one nation,
under God . . ."

"A nation is a single country," says Michael. "Many different kinds of people make up our country."

"indivisible . . ."

"Our nation can't be split apart," says Danny.

"with liberty and justice for all."

"Everyone here has freedom to live
the way they want to," says Erica.
"And we're all treated equally under the law."

"The Pledge of Allegiance is a promise to be true to the United States of America," says Ms. Francis.